TODAY'S SUPERSTARS

Will Smith

By Joe McGowan

Gareth Stevens
Publishing

Please visit our web site at www.garethstevens.com.
For a free catalog describing Gareth Stevens Publishing's list of high-quality books, call 1-800-542-2595 (USA) or 1-800-387-3178 (Canada).
Gareth Stevens Publishing's fax: 1-877-542-2596

Library of Congress Cataloging-in-Publication Data
McGowan, Joe.
     Will Smith / by Joe McGowan.
       p. cm. — (Today's superstars)
    Includes bibliographical references and index.
    ISBN-10: 1-4339-2380-7   ISBN-13: 978-1-4339-2380-7 (lib. bdg.)
    ISBN-10: 1-4339-2376-9   ISBN-13: 978-1-4339-2376-0 (soft cover)
    1. Smith, Will, 1968– —Juvenile literature. 2. Actors—United States—Biography—
    Juvenile literature. I. Title.
    PN2287.S612M43 2009
    791.4302'8092—dc22   2009003208

This edition first published in 2010 by
Gareth Stevens Publishing
A Weekly Reader® Company
1 Reader's Digest Road
Pleasantville, NY 10570-7000 USA

Copyright © 2010 by Gareth Stevens, Inc.

Executive Managing Editor: Lisa M. Herrington
Senior Designer: Keith Plechaty

Produced by Editorial Directions, Inc.

Art Direction and Page Production: The Design Lab

Photo credits: cover, title page AP Photo/Mark J. Terrill; p. 4 AP Photo/Laura Rauch; p. 7 AP Photo/Paul White; p. 8 AP Photo/Mark J. Terrill; p. 9 AP Photo/Jan Bauer; p. 10 and 46 Chris Haston/NBCU Photo Bank via AP Images; p.12 Yearbook Library; p. 13 AP Photo; p. 14 AP Photo/Achmad Ibrahim; p. 15 Andresr/Shuterstock; p. 16 and 40 David Drapkin/ImageDirect/Getty Images; p. 17 AP Photo; p. 18, 20, 21 Chris Haston/NBCU Photo Bank via AP Images; 20th Century Fox Film Corp. All right reserved. Courtesy Everett Collection; p. 24 Pictorial Press Ltd/Alamy; p. 25 Matt Campbell/AFP/Getty Images; p. 26 Columbia Pictures/courtesy Everett Collection; p. 27 Moneta Sleet Jr./Ebony Collection via AP Images; p. 28 AP Photo/Matt Sayles; p. 30 Columbia Pictures/Photofest; p. 31 AP Photo/Franka Bruns; p. 32 Warner Bros./courtesy Everett Collection; p. 33 AP Photo Matt Sayles; p. 34 John Shearer/WireImage/Getty Images; p. 36 and 41 AP Photo/Chris Pizzello; p. 37 AP Photo/Lefteris Pitarakis; p. 38 AP Photo/Matt Sayles/Jae C. Hong; p. 39 AP Photo/MJ Kim; p. 48 Kathy Kneeland

Printed in the United States of America

1 2 3 4 5 6 7 8 9 14 13 12 11 10 09

Contents

Words in the glossary appear in **bold** type the first time they are used in the text.

"In my mind, I've always been a Hollywood A-list superstar. **Y'ALL JUST DIDN'T KNOW IT YET."**

—Will Smith

Will Smith arrives at the Academy Awards in 2002 with his wife, Jada Pinkett Smith.

Chapter 1

A Confident Superstar

In March 2002, Will Smith attended the **Academy Awards** ceremony in Los Angeles, California. He had already won awards for his work in the music industry and on TV, but never an Academy Award. Also known as the Oscar, the award is the entertainment industry's highest honor. That year, Smith was nominated as best actor for his work in *Ali*, a movie about the life of the boxer Muhammad Ali.

About his Oscar nomination, Smith said, "In my mind, I've always been a Hollywood A-list superstar. Y'all just didn't know it yet." With his first Oscar nomination, he was on his way to the top.

A Member of the Club

Smith is one of a small group of performers who have been successful in different types of entertainment. There seems to be nothing he can't do. As a rap singer and musician, he had early success with popular hits such as "Girls Ain't Nothing but Trouble" and "Parents Just Don't Understand."

He also starred in a hit TV **sitcom**, called *The Fresh Prince of Bel-Air*. "It's a whole different thing being an actor," Smith told *GQ* magazine. "A rapper is about being completely true to yourself. Being an actor is about changing who you are."

TRUE OR FALSE?

In 1998, *People* magazine named Smith to its list of the Most Beautiful People in the World.

For answers, see page 46.

All About Will

Name: Willard Christopher Smith Jr.

Birth date: September 25, 1968

Birthplace: Philadelphia, Pennsylvania

Height: 6 feet 2 inches (188 centimeters)

Current homes: Miami, Florida; Stockholm, Sweden; Philadelphia, Pennsylvania

Family: Jada (wife), Willard III and Jaden (sons), Willow (daughter)

Parents: Willard Christopher Smith Sr. and Caroline

Siblings: Pam and Ellen (sisters); Harry (brother). Ellen and Harry are twins.

The Big Screen

In 1992, Smith began to act in motion pictures. It didn't take him long to become a superstar. In less than 10 years, he was commanding multimillion-dollar salaries for starring in movies. Despite his riches, he has remained a regular guy. "He's the biggest movie star on the planet, but he's still the same Will, the same good guy," his rap partner, DJ Jazzy Jeff, told *People* magazine.

▲ Smith waves to fans while promoting a film in Spain.

A Star With Charm

Smith is famous for his charm. Since his childhood, his friendly personality and sense of humor have helped him stand out. They've also made him popular with moviegoers of all races and ages.

Fact File

In 1992, Smith made $50,000 in his first movie, *Where the Day Takes You.* Today he typically earns $20 million per film and gets a portion of ticket sales.

At the Top

Smith is also a smart businessman. In 2007, *Entertainment Weekly* magazine named him one of the smartest people in Hollywood. Smith has built a successful career that keeps growing.

He has nonstop energy and excitement about his work. With each business decision, he focuses on his goal to stay at the top of the entertainment industry. Smith told *Time* magazine, "It's an addiction for me to see where my artistry can touch people."

TRUE OR FALSE?

Smith has said that if he hadn't become a performer, he would have been a lawyer.

In Good Company

Here are Hollywood's highest-paid actors, according to money earned from June 2007 to May 2008:

1. Will Smith	$80 million
2. Johnny Depp	$72 million
3. Mike Myers	$55 million
3. Eddie Murphy	$55 million
5. Leonardo DiCaprio	$45 million

Source: *Forbes* magazine

A Happy Man

Smith may already be a success, but he continues to look for new challenges. Being a superstar has given him the ability to take risks. Instead of playing it safe portraying one kind of character, he has accepted many different types of roles.

Over the years, he has never backed down from taking a chance. Like everyone, Smith has succeeded at some challenges and failed at others. In recent years, his record of success has been unmatched by most actors in Hollywood.

Today, Smith is just as famous for his success as he is for his extraordinary talent and charm. "I just love living," he said. "I'm glad every single day. I think that even the camera can feel that I'm a happy man."

Fact File

From 2002 to 2008, Smith starred in eight movies in a row that have made more than $100 million at the box office. No other actor in history beats that record.

▶ Smith performs for a crowd in Germany in 2002.

9

"The first step is that you have **TO SAY THAT YOU CAN.**"

—Will Smith

Even in his younger days, Will Smith had energy and star quality.

Chapter 2

A Kid From the 'Hood

Willard Christopher Smith Jr. was born on September 25, 1968, in West Philadelphia, Pennsylvania. His father worked seven days a week running a refrigerator company. Will's mother worked in the local school system.

Will's father expected a lot from him and his brother and two sisters. Will recalled his dad saying, "Don't you ever tell me there's something you can't do."

Today, Will Smith says he inherited his father's commitment to hard work and his mother's belief in education. "Every problem I have ever had, I found the answer in a book," he said.

 Will Smith poses for a high school photo.

A Melting Pot

Will's childhood neighborhood was a melting pot of **cultures**. Many different types of people called it home. Jews lived alongside Muslims. Will's family attended a Baptist church, but he went to a Catholic school. Most of Will's schoolmates were white, but the majority of his friends were black. The diverse cultures of Will's community helped him develop his comedy. "I started looking for the jokes that were equally [funny] across the board," he said.

Will was a smart kid. He attended a middle school for high-achieving students. He went on to Overbrook High School, where he was a good student and had many friends. His teachers and classmates nicknamed him "Prince." They said that Will's charming personality always got him out of trouble.

College Bound?

Early in Will's career, a rumor spread that he had turned down a scholarship to the Massachusetts Institute of Technology (MIT). MIT is an elite university near Boston, Massachusetts. Smith put the rumor to rest when he told an interviewer that his mother encouraged him to apply, but he never did. "I had pretty high SAT scores and they [MIT] needed black kids, so I probably could have gotten in," he said. "But I had no intention of going to college."

TRUE OR FALSE?

Will Smith has Native American ancestors.

Famous Graduates

Will studied at Overbrook High School on Lancaster Avenue in Philadelphia. Founded in 1924, the public school has a long history of educating the city's teenagers. Many have gone on to make it big. Besides Will, basketball great Wilt "The Stilt" Chamberlain and U.S. congressman Chaka Fattah attended Overbrook.

▶ **Wilt Chamberlain was one of the greatest players in the history of the NBA.**

Rap Along

Philadelphia is known around the world for its contributions to all kinds of music. This includes classical music, jazz, R&B, and opera. Long before MTV, young people tuned in to *American Bandstand*. This TV program was hosted by Dick Clark and broadcast from Philadelphia. The city also played a role in the early development of hip-hop. Philadelphia has produced many rap artists, including Will Smith, the Roots, and Schoolly D, and the R&B group Boyz II Men.

◄ **Members of Boyz II Men perform at a concert in Asia.**

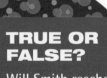

TRUE OR FALSE?

Will Smith reached his adult height of 6 feet 2 inches (188 cm) when he was 16 years old.

Let the Music Play

In high school, Will also loved music, a hobby he had enjoyed for years. He started rapping at age 12 and especially liked hip-hop stars such as Grandmaster Flash. Will often performed his music at friends' parties. In time, he developed a clean, comic style that was popular with his pals.

A Party to Remember

When Will was 16 years old, he met someone who would help turn his love of music into a multimillion-dollar success. At a party in Philadelphia, the always-clowning Will played a practical joke on his friends. Another partygoer, Jeff Townes, who is also known as DJ Jazzy Jeff, thought Will was funny and wanted to meet him.

A Rap Team Is Born

Will and Jeff quickly became close friends and started playing music together. Jeff had been creating tunes since he was 10 years old. The new team was called DJ Jazzy Jeff & the Fresh Prince. Jeff mixed and scratched the music, while Will wrote and rapped clever rhymes.

Fact File

As a professional rapper, Will Smith changed his nickname to Fresh Prince. He wanted to highlight his clean style of hip-hop music.

Will's Favorites

✔ **Food:** Philly cheesesteak

✔ **Board game:** Chess

✔ **Sport:** Golf

✔ **Spectator sport:** Professional wrestling

✔ **Colors:** Red and black

Rapping to Their Own Beat

Smith and Townes were determined to be successful. Their style was the opposite of gangsta rap, which typically encouraged violence and harmful behavior. In 1987, Smith and Townes released their first album, *Rock the House*. In the single, "Girls Ain't Nothing but Trouble," Smith advises "homeboys" to avoid young women.

Losing It All

Smith was still in high school when *Rock the House* was released. He was suddenly a millionaire. However, the young rapper spent money unwisely and failed to pay his taxes. He nearly lost everything. Instead of giving up, he remembered some advice from his grandmother. She said, "Don't let failure go to your heart and don't let success go to your head."

Fact File

"Girls Ain't Nothing but Trouble" sampled the music from the theme song to the 1960s TV show *I Dream of Jeannie.*

▼ *Rock the House* turned Smith and Townes into hip-hop superstars.

By the Numbers: *He's the DJ, I'm the Rapper*

1 Grammy Award ("Parents Just Don't Understand")

18 Number of songs on the album

1988 First released

3 million+ Copies sold

Success on the Rebound

Smith released more hit albums and was able to rebuild his fortune. The album *He's the DJ, I'm the Rapper* broke records by selling more than 3 million copies in the United States. In 1989, Smith and Townes won the first-ever **Grammy Award** for a rap performance.

More fame was headed Smith's way. In the video for the song "Parents Just Don't Understand," Smith is trying to avoid his parents' rules by sleeping late and pretending to be sick. The video inspired **producers** to develop a TV show for him. His future looked bright.

▲ In 1989, DJ Jazzy Jeff & the Fresh Prince won two American Music Awards.

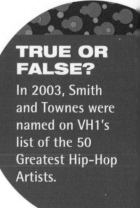

TRUE OR FALSE?

In 2003, Smith and Townes were named on VH1's list of the 50 Greatest Hip-Hop Artists.

"Will Smith is A BREAKOUT STAR."

—NBC press release, 1990

Smith performs in an episode from the first season of *The Fresh Prince of Bel-Air.*

Chapter 3

A Prince Goes to Hollywood

In 1990, Smith moved to Los Angeles for a new challenge. The popular rap singer was already at the top of the music world. Smith's success led to an offer to star in a TV series based on his life. The sitcom was called *The Fresh Prince of Bel-Air*.

The character Smith played in the show was remarkably like the real-life Will. The character had grown up on the streets of Philadelphia, like Smith. He had moved to Los Angeles, where he lived in a world of wealth surrounded by mansions, sports cars, and swimming pools. He sang rap music and used his charm to get out of trouble. Even the character's name, William "Will" Smith, was the same.

A Hit in the Making

The Fresh Prince of Bel-Air was a hit. Each week, fans tuned in to watch Smith clash with his rich, stuffy relatives, the Bankses. The upper-class family wanted to teach Smith to be sophisticated, but he had other ideas. According to the theme song, Smith would rather "chill out, max, and relax."

Critics also enjoyed the show. A writer for *Entertainment Weekly* magazine said Will was a "TV natural." The NBC network predicted the new sitcom would be a "sure-fire hit" and called Smith a "breakout star." NBC was right. *The Fresh Prince of Bel-Air* ran for six seasons, with a total of 148 episodes.

Fact File

Smith and DJ Jazzy Jeff wrote the theme song for *The Fresh Prince of Bel-Air.*

▲ Smith appears in a scene with Alfonso Ribiero, who played his cousin Carlton.

Learning His Lines

Acting didn't come naturally to Smith at first. He told a reporter on the TV show *60 Minutes* that during the early days of *The Fresh Prince of Bel-Air*, he was clueless about filming and learning his lines. He said he often memorized everyone's lines. During filming, he would mouth the other actors' lines as they were speaking them. "Will was so intent," said the show's creator, Andy Borowitz.

A Launch to Superstardom

The Fresh Prince of Bel-Air gave Smith a chance to show off his comedy talent. Fans loved his friendly charm and good looks. He won a Kids' Choice Award as favorite TV actor in 1991. The show was honored with an **NAACP** Image Award for outstanding comedy series in 1992. The Image Awards are given to people of color for their work in entertainment and literature.

Smith also attracted Hollywood's attention. The TV star began to receive offers to act in movies. *The Fresh Prince of Bel-Air* would be another step on his path to superstardom. The rapper from Philadelphia was on his way to the top of the entertainment world.

▶ Smith poses with the rest of the cast from *The Fresh Prince of Bel-Air.*

21

"I want to be the biggest movie **STAR IN THE WORLD.**"

—Will Smith

Smith stars as Captain Steven Hiller in the 1996 film *Independence Day*.

Chapter 4

The Making of a Movie Idol

Smith began to act in movies while working on the TV sitcom. In 1992, he made his first movie, called *Where the Day Takes You*. It was about teenage runaways living on the streets of Los Angeles. Smith earned $50,000 for his work. He was listed at the bottom of the movie poster's cast list. Still, it was a beginning.

The next year, Smith acted in *Made in America*, starring comedian Whoopi Goldberg. He played Tea Cake Walters, the best friend of Goldberg's movie daughter. It was another comedy role, not unlike the role he played on TV.

 ▲ Martin Lawrence was Smith's costar in *Bad Boys.*

Drama and Action

In the dramatic movie *Six Degrees of Separation*, Smith portrayed a young con man. His character tricked a wealthy New York couple into giving him food, money, and a place to stay. Movie critics praised Smith's dramatic acting.

Give Me the Money

Smith's first big moneymaking movie was 1995's *Bad Boys*. The action thriller was the first film to star two African Americans in the top roles. It made $141 million worldwide, proving that Smith was a hit at the box office. He was laying a firm foundation for his film career.

TRUE OR FALSE?

Smith received his first Academy Award nomination for his role in *Six Degrees of Separation.*

The Road to Mega-Success

Smith's goal was to become "the biggest movie star in the world." To do that, he studied the top 10 moneymaking films of all time. He and James Lassiter, his business partner, looked for hints about what moviegoers and studios enjoyed most. Smith told a writer for *Time*, "We realized that 10 out of the 10 had special effects. Nine out of 10 had special effects with creatures. Eight out of 10 had special effects with creatures and a love story."

Then Smith and Lassiter developed a plan for success. Smith would accept a role only if he and Lassiter thought it would be a step toward superstardom.

Fact File

Smith turned down the role of Neo in *The Matrix*. According to his new plan for success, he didn't think it was the right role at the right time.

Music Man

Smith has continued his successful music career, even after becoming a film star. Here are some of his hit singles and their top positions in the United States:

Song (Year)	Position
"Gettin' Jiggy Wit It" (1998)	1
"Just the Two of Us" (1998)	20
"Miami" (1998)	17
"Wild, Wild West" (1999)	1
"Will 2K" (1999)	25
"Switch" (2005)	7

Source: Billboard

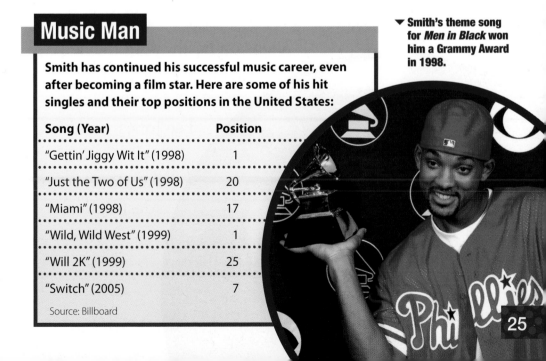

▼ Smith's theme song for *Men in Black* won him a Grammy Award in 1998.

Launching the Plan

In July 1996, Smith starred in the **science-fiction** adventure, *Independence Day*. He played Captain Steve Hiller, a pilot in the U.S. Marines. In the movie, Smith's character helps save the world from an invasion by space aliens.

Independence Day was a blockbuster hit. It made more money than any other movie that year, earning more than $104 million during its first week alone. Smith had taken his first step toward superstardom.

Aliens, Part Two

Smith's next movie was *Men in Black*. It was another major success. He played Agent Jay, a member of a secret organization that watches the activities of aliens on Earth. With the help of another agent, Kay, played by Tommy Lee Jones, Smith's character saves the planet from destruction.

▼ Tommy Lee Jones and Smith star in the 1997 film *Men in Black*.

"The Greatest"

The boxer Cassius Marcellus Clay Jr., also known as Muhammad Ali, was born in Louisville, Kentucky, in 1942. He was a great athlete. As a young boxer, Ali won a gold medal at the 1960 Olympics. In 1964, he became the world heavyweight champ. "I am the greatest," he said. He is still widely considered one of the greatest boxers of all time.

Throughout his life, Ali also fought against **racism** in the United States. "Hating people because of their color is wrong," he said. "It doesn't matter what color does the hating. It's just plain wrong." In 2000, *Time* named him a "hero and **icon**" of the 20th century.

▶ Muhammad Ali's life story was a great inspiration to Smith.

A Giant of a Role

In 2001, Smith took on his biggest acting challenge yet. That year, he starred in *Ali*, a movie about the boxer Muhammad Ali. Smith worked hard preparing for the film. He even trained with professional boxers. Critics said Smith gave his "strongest performance" in the movie. He received an Academy Award nomination as best actor.

TRUE OR FALSE?

Will Smith speaks Spanish and German fluently.

"If you're not willing to work hard, LET SOMEONE ELSE DO IT."
—Will Smith

Smith has become good friends with fellow actor Tom Cruise.

Chapter 5

More Than an Actor

Smith's hit movies have made him a major star in Hollywood. With each film, he has become more powerful in the entertainment industry. In 2006, Smith was included on *Premiere* magazine's list of the most powerful people in Hollywood. Smith was the second-highest-ranking actor on the list, behind Tom Cruise.

His success has allowed him to try new roles in different kinds of movies. In 2000, he starred in *The Legend of Bagger Vance*, playing a traveler who helps a professional golfer regain his confidence. In 2004, he did an animated movie, *Shark Tale*. Smith was the voice of Oscar, a young fish who pretends he killed a gangster shark.

Will's Way

Smith says his career has taken a lot of work. "If you're not willing to work hard, let someone else do it," he says. "I'd rather be with someone who does a horrible job, but gives 110 percent, than with someone who does a good job and gives 60 percent."

▲ Smith and Kevin James star in the 2005 comedy *Hitch*.

A New Type of Role

In the 2005 film *Hitch*, Smith played a character who brings couples together. It was the first time he starred in a romantic comedy. Fans loved it. The success of *Hitch* confirmed Smith's solid position in Hollywood.

Smith doesn't let Hollywood's glamour influence him. He likes to quote Will Rogers, a famous American performer in the 1930s. Rogers said, "Too many people spend money they haven't earned to buy things they don't want to impress people they don't like."

TRUE OR FALSE?

Smith is listed in the *Guinness World Records*.

Keeping It in the Family

In 2006, Smith starred in *The Pursuit of Happyness*. It is based on a true story. He plays Chris Gardner, a homeless man who works to rebuild his life and takes care of his son. Smith's real-life eight-year-old son, Jaden, played his son in the movie. *The Pursuit of Happyness* earned Smith his second Academy Award nomination for best actor.

Fact File

Smith's 2004 science-fiction film, *I, Robot*, was a huge success. It earned nearly $350 million worldwide.

A Helping Hand

The real-life Chris Gardner was born in 1954 in Milwaukee, Wisconsin. He grew up in poverty. When his son was born in 1981, Gardner vowed to give him a better life. Gardner became a trainee in a financial company. He and his son were homeless on the streets of San Francisco. With help from charities, Gardner was able to improve his life. Today, he is a millionaire businessman who helps homeless people.

Initially, Gardner was unsure if an action star like Smith should portray him. But Gardner's daughter said, "If he can play Muhammad Ali, he can play you!"

▲ Will Smith and Chris Gardner appear at the German premiere of *The Pursuit of Happyness*.

▲ Will Smith stars as Robert Neville in *I Am Legend.*

Fair Pay

Smith is one of the highest-paid actors in the world. According to the business magazine *Forbes*, he earned an estimated $80 million in 2008 alone. The magazine projected that for every dollar Smith earns, his movies make 10 dollars at the box office. This means the studios that paid for the movies make huge **profits**. No wonder movie studios love to work with Smith.

Back to Basics

In 2007, Smith returned to science-fiction and action films. That year, he acted in *I Am Legend*. His character is the last surviving man in New York City. He is a scientist working to find a cure for a deadly virus. In 2008, Smith starred in the action comedy *Hancock*. He plays a superhero with a drinking problem. He's too lazy to help people and just wants to be left alone.

Behind the Scenes

Smith's success has also given him the ability to work behind the camera. In the late 1990s, Smith and James Lassiter founded a production company. It's called Overbrook Entertainment, named after Smith's high school.

The company makes films, music, and television shows. The TV series *All of Us* was produced by Overbrook. It's based on the lives of Will and his wife, Jada Pinkett Smith. Overbrook has also produced the music for some of Smith's movies, including *Hitch* and *Men in Black II*.

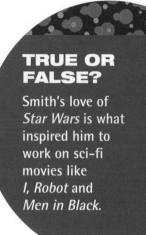

TRUE OR FALSE?

Smith's love of *Star Wars* is what inspired him to work on sci-fi movies like *I, Robot* and *Men in Black*.

Who's the Boss?

Big-time actors may seem to call the shots in Hollywood. But, as Will Smith knows, producers are the real bosses. Their main role is to raise money for a movie, album, or TV show. They then make sure the money is spent wisely. Producers plan how to advertise a movie and sell tickets. A producer's job also includes hiring directors. Directors oversee the making of an album or the filming of a movie or TV show. They work with actors and film crews.

▶ Famed director Steven Spielberg was the executive producer of the *Men in Black* movies.

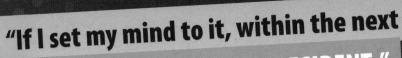

"If I set my mind to it, within the next **15 YEARS I WOULD BE PRESIDENT.**"

—Will Smith

Will Smith poses with his family at the premiere of *Hancock.*

Chapter 6

A Model Citizen

Will Smith is a role model for many people. As a dad, he gets his greatest pleasure from his family. "I really believe that a man and a woman together, raising a family, is the purest form of happiness we can experience," he said.

Like all families, Smith's has faced some challenges. In 1992, he married his first wife, Sheree Zampino. The couple had met at the filming of a TV series called *A Different World*. Will and Sheree had a son, Willard Smith III, nicknamed "Trey." In 1995, the couple divorced.

It was a difficult time for Smith. But before long, Smith would have a new love in his life—and a new start.

A New Beginning

Will Smith first met Jada Pinkett in 1990. That year, the actress **auditioned** for the role of Smith's girlfriend in *The Fresh Prince of Bel-Air*. Jada didn't get the job, but she and Will eventually began to date. The couple married in 1997. They are considered one of Hollywood's happiest couples. "I honestly believe there is no woman for me but Jada," said Smith.

A Family Business

Jada and Will have two children. Their son, Jaden Christopher, was born in 1998. His sister, Willow, was born in 2000. Like their brother Jaden, Willow and Trey have performed with their celebrity dad. Trey appeared in a music video with Will. Willow played his daughter in *I Am Legend.*

◀ Will and Jada have been married since 1997.

The Role of Race

Throughout his career, Smith has been a role model for African Americans. He has even won awards from the NAACP and **BET** for setting a positive image of success. "I love being black in America, and especially being black in Hollywood," he has said proudly.

◀ Smith takes part in the 90th birthday celebration for former South African president Nelson Mandela.

Beyond the Family

Will Smith also finds time to help people in need. He and Jada assisted in relief efforts for the victims of Hurricane Katrina. In 2005, the monster storm destroyed parts of Louisiana, Mississippi, Florida, and Texas. The same year, Smith hosted a *Live 8* concert in his hometown of Philadelphia. The event helped raise money for people in need around the world.

TRUE OR FALSE?

Before meeting Jada, Will Smith briefly dated singer Mariah Carey.

Smith also supports community organizations. One group in Philadelphia teaches kids martial arts. "If you give me a problem, I'll find a solution," he says.

A Presidential Role?

Will Smith supported Barack Obama for president. During the campaign, Obama said that if a movie is ever made about his life, he'd want Smith to play him. "He has the ears," Obama joked. Both Obama and Smith have often poked fun at themselves for having big ears.

▲ Could Smith's resemblance to President Barack Obama land him another major role one day?

Youth in Politics

Smith has encouraged young people to develop an interest in their country and its leaders. In 1993, he hosted the Presidential Inaugural Celebration for Youth in Washington, D.C. The event celebrated the beginning of President Bill Clinton's years in the White House.

In 2008, Will and Jada participated in the Head of State "Living the Dream" Youth-Nation Inaugural Ball. It honored the involvement of millions of youths in Barack Obama's 2008 presidential campaign. It also celebrated Martin Luther King Jr.'s dream of equality for African Americans.

Fact File

Smith appeared in a public service announcement to encourage people to vote in the 2008 election.

Art Reflecting Life

Obama and Smith have discussed the idea of making a film about the 2008 presidential election. If it's made, the movie could be a rehearsal for Smith. He has hinted at a career in politics. "If I set my mind to it, within the next 15 years I would be president," Smith said.

A Prince Becomes a King

Smith may one day enter politics. For now, his focus remains on making megahit movies. In 2008, he starred in *Seven Pounds*, a drama about an unhappy government worker. Next up, Smith plans to take on the ancient world. He'll produce and star in *The Last Pharaoh*. It's a movie about King Taharqa, who ruled Egypt from 690 to 664 B.C.

▼ Smith arrives at the *Seven Pounds* premiere in London.

Smith has been successful in all kinds of movies — science fiction, thrillers, comedies, and dramas. If his previous films offer any clue, the rapper from Philadelphia will be a megastar in the ancient world as well.

Time Line

1968 Willard Christopher Smith Jr. is born on September 25, in Philadelphia, Pennsylvania.

1987 Smith, known as "Fresh Prince," and DJ Jazzy Jeff release *Rock the House*.

1989 Smith and DJ Jazzy Jeff win the first-ever Grammy Award for best rap performance.

1990 Smith stars in *The Fresh Prince of Bel-Air* TV series.

1992 Smith marries his first wife, Sheree Zampino. (They divorce in 1995.) Will appears in his first movie, *Where the Day Takes You*.

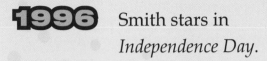

1996   Smith stars in *Independence Day*.

1997   Smith and Jada Pinkett-Smith marry. *Men in Black* is released.

2002   Smith gets his first Academy Award nomination for his work in the movie *Ali*.

2005   *Hitch*, Smith's first romantic comedy, is released.

2007   Smith earns a second Academy Award nomination for *The Pursuit of Happyness*.

2008   Smith sets a record with the movie *Hancock*. It was his eighth consecutive movie that earned more than $100 million.

Glossary

Academy Awards: the highest honors in the film industry

auditioned: tried out for a role in a movie, play, or TV show

BET (Black Entertainment Television): a cable TV network based in Washington, D.C., that is targeted to young African Americans living in cities

critics: people whose job is to give their opinions about movies, plays, TV shows, or music

cultures: the symbols, heroes, arts, behavior, and beliefs that unite groups

Grammy Award: the highest award in the recording industry

icon: an important and lasting symbol of a time or place; a person who receives great attention and devotion

NAACP (National Association for the Advancement of Colored People): an organization that helps ethnic groups in the United States defend their legal and personal rights

producers: people who are in charge of making movies, TV shows, and music recordings

profits: the money that remains after the cost of making something is subtracted

racism: hatred or distrust based on someone's ethnic background

science-fiction: having to do with a type of book or movie that uses real or future scientific discoveries and technology as part of its story

sitcom: (short for "situation comedy") a TV comedy series that has the same characters in each episode